COVENTRY LIBRARIES

**Please return this book on or before
the last date stamped below.** ·

CENTRAL

To renew this book take it to any of
the City Libraries before
the date due for return

Coventry City Council

ENGLAND WORLD CUP SONGBOOK

PUBLISHED BY
WISE PUBLICATIONS
14-15 BERNERS STREET, LONDON, W1T 3LJ, UK.

EXCLUSIVE DISTRIBUTORS:
MUSIC SALES LIMITED
DISTRIBUTION CENTRE, NEWMARKET ROAD,
BURY ST EDMUNDS, SUFFOLK, IP33 3YB, UK.

MUSIC SALES PTY LIMITED
120 ROTHSCHILD AVENUE, ROSEBERY,
NSW 2018, AUSTRALIA.

ORDER NO. AM986150
ISBN 1-84609-627-8
THIS BOOK © COPYRIGHT 2006 WISE PUBLICATIONS,
A DIVISION OF MUSIC SALES LIMITED.

EDITED BY DAVID WESTON & ANN FARMER.
MUSIC PROCESSED BY PAUL EWERS MUSIC DESIGN.
COVER PHOTOGRAPHS COURTESY OF LFI & REUTERS/CORBIS.

PRINTED IN THE EU.

YOUR GUARANTEE OF QUALITY:
AS PUBLISHERS, WE STRIVE TO PRODUCE EVERY BOOK
TO THE HIGHEST COMMERCIAL STANDARDS.

THE BOOK HAS BEEN CAREFULLY DESIGNED TO MINIMISE AWKWARD PAGE TURNS
AND TO MAKE PLAYING FROM IT A REAL PLEASURE. PARTICULAR CARE HAS BEEN GIVEN
TO SPECIFYING ACID-FREE, NEUTRAL-SIZED PAPER MADE FROM PULPS
WHICH HAVE NOT BEEN ELEMENTAL CHLORINE BLEACHED.

THIS PULP IS FROM FARMED SUSTAINABLE FORESTS AND
WAS PRODUCED WITH SPECIAL REGARD FOR THE ENVIRONMENT.

THROUGHOUT, THE PRINTING AND BINDING HAVE BEEN PLANNED
TO ENSURE A STURDY, ATTRACTIVE PUBLICATION WHICH SHOULD GIVE
YEARS OF ENJOYMENT.

IF YOUR COPY FAILS TO MEET OUR HIGH STANDARDS, PLEASE INFORM US
AND WE WILL GLADLY REPLACE IT.

WWW.MUSICSALES.COM

Wise Publications
part of The Music Sales Group
LONDON / NEW YORK / PARIS / SYDNEY / COPENHAGEN / BERLIN / MADRID / TOKYO

The Time Of Our Lives

Official Song Of The 2006 FIFA World Cup

Words & Music by
Jörgen Elofsson

6

Eat My Goal

Words & Music by
Anthony Chapman, Jim Burke & Stephen Harcourt

Say ho___ (Ho)___ Say

May or may not be a-mused; no ask me,___ 'cos me plain be-mused.⎫ Say
and with the mind of a les - ser spot-ted bloke. That won't make you choke.⎭

ho.___ (Ho)__ Say ho wo. (Ho wo) Eat my goal. (Eat my goal) Say

eat my goal (Eat my goal) Say ho.___ (Ho)__ Say ho wo. (Ho wo)

1.

Eat my goal. (Eat my goal) Say eat my goal. (Eat my goal)

2.

eat my goal. (Eat my goal) Say

Who Do You Think You Are Kidding Jurgen Klinsmann?

Based on 'Who Do You Think You Are Kidding Mr Hitler?'

Words & Music by
Derek Taverner & Jimmy Perry

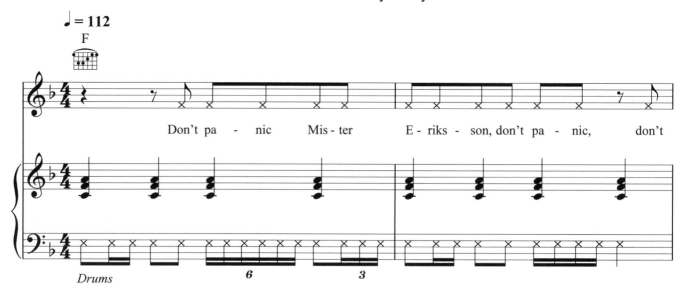

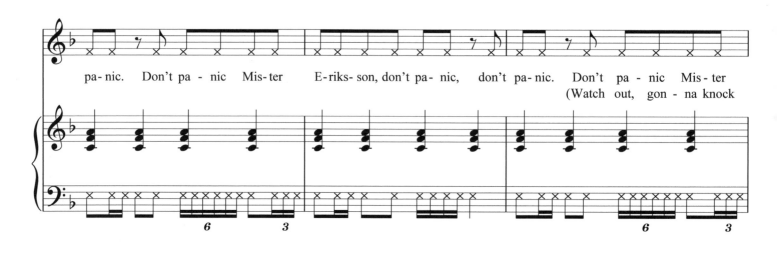

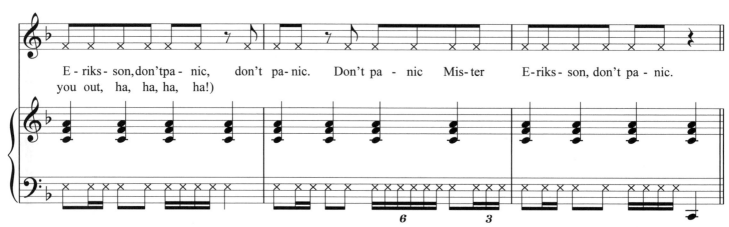

15

Ri - o, Ne - ville, Ter - ry, Ow - en and the Gold - en One, work - ing for the Swe - dish mas - ter
Ma - ny coun - tries play - ing for their na - tional pride and joy, Eng - land's got a se - cret wea - pon, he

Mis - ter E - riks - son. So watch out Jur - gen Klins - man, you have met your match in us. If
ain't no stu - pid boy. So watch out Jur - gen Klins - man now, your team will send you ma - nic.

you think you can crush us we're a - fraid you've missed the bus. } 'Cos who do you think you are
Here's some good a - vice for you... "Ein, zwei, drei, get rea - dy!" }

kid - ding Jur - gen Klins - man if you think Old Eng - land's done?

16

N.C.

There's a player down, it's the German Captain, Michael Ballack.   Oh dear, he's injured.

Drums

What are they going to do now?   Everybody knows the German's have only got one Ballack!   (Ya know what

I mean Jurgen? Ha, ha, ha, ha!)   With   the

crowd   on   our   side   and   the   ball   at   our   feet,   there's
boys   from   Eng   -   land,   they   nev   -   er   give   up.   So

on - ly one re - sult, you are gon - na get beat. The
did - n't you know guv, it's Wayne's World Cup. It's a

boys of six - ty six, they're still a - round.___ They
Wayne's world, Wayne's world, Wayne's world cup.___ It's a

D.S. al Coda

give us pow - er from a - bove to win their world cup crown. The
Wayne's world, Wayne's world, Wayne's world cup.

Coda

Gm⁷   C⁷   F

(Ya know what I mean Jurgen?   Ha, ha, ha, ha!)

18

1966: ENGLAND CAPTAIN BOBBY MOORE (1941-93) RAISES THE JULES RIMET TROPHY IN THE AIR AS HE IS CARRIED ON TEAM-MATES,
GEOFF HURST AND RAY WILSON'S SHOULDERS, FOLLOWING THEIR 4-2 VICTORY OVER WEST GERMANY IN THE WORLD CUP FINAL AT WEMBLEY
PHOTO: CENTRAL PRESS/GETTY IMAGES

ENGLAND GOALKEEPER GORDON BANKS MAKES A REMARKABLE SAVE FROM A HEADER BY PELE OF BRAZIL
DURING THEIR FIRST ROUND MATCH IN THE WORLD CUP AT GUADALAJARA, MEXICO, JUNE 1970. BRAZIL WENT ON TO WIN 1-0

1989: TERRY BUTCHER OF ENGLAND IS COVERED IN BLOOD
DURING A WORLD CUP QUALIFYING MATCH IN SWEDEN. THE MATCH ENDED IN A 0-0 DRAW
PHOTO: DAVID CANNON/ALLSPORT/GETTY IMAGES

4 JULY 1990: GARY LINEKER OF ENGLAND CELEBRATES AFTER SCORING THE EQUALISER AGAINST WEST GERMANY IN THEIR WORLD CUP SEMI FINAL MATCH PLAYED IN THE DELLE ALPI STADIUM IN TURIN. THE MATCH WAS A 1-1 DRAW AFTER EXTRA TIME, BUT WEST GERMANY WON THE PENALTY SHOOT OUT 4-3

4 JULY 1990: PAUL GASCOIGNE OF ENGLAND IS BROUGHT TO TEARS AFTER RECEIVING
A YELLOW CARD IN THE WORLD CUP SEMI-FINAL MATCH AGAINST WEST GERMANY
PHOTO: GETTY IMAGES

8 JUNE 1996: ALAN SHEARER OF ENGLAND CLEBRATES AFTER SCORING THE OPENING GOAL OF THE TOURNAMENT DURING THE EUROPEAN FOOTBALL CHAMPIONSHIP GAME BETWEEN ENGLAND AND SWITZERLAND AT WEMBLEY STADIUM, LONDON. THE GAME ENDED IN A 1-1 DRAW

PHOTO: SHAUN BOTTERILL/ALLSPORT UK/GETTY IMAGES

22 JUNE 1996: STUART PEARCE OF ENGLAND CELEBRATES AFTER SCORING HIS PENALTY DURING THE EUROPEAN FOOTBALL CHAMPIONSHIP MATCH
BETWEEN ENGLAND AND SPAIN AT WEMBLEY STADIUM, LONDON. ENGLAND WON THE MATCH AFTER EXTRA TIME IN A PENALTY SHOOT-OUT 4-2

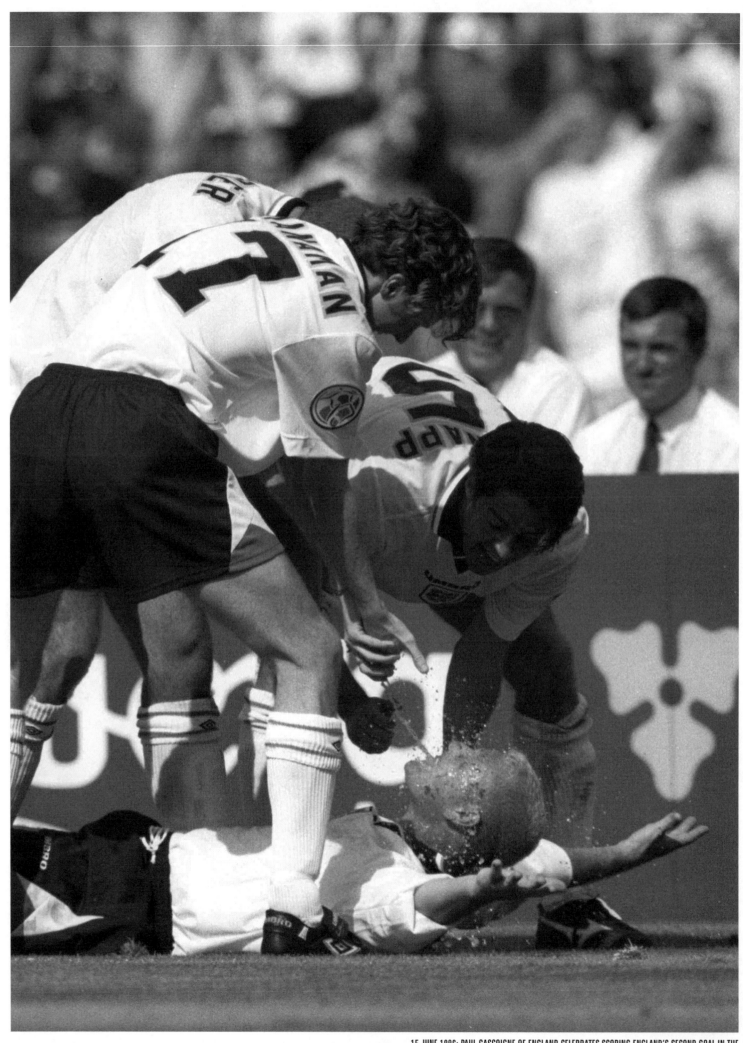

15 JUNE 1996: PAUL GASCOIGNE OF ENGLAND CELEBRATES SCORING ENGLAND'S SECOND GOAL IN THE
ENGLAND V SCOTLAND MATCH IN GROUP A OF THE EUROPEAN FOOTBALL CHAMPIONSHIPS AT WEMBLEY. ENGLAND BEAT SCOTLAND 2-0

1 SEPTEMBER 2001: MICHAEL OWEN OF ENGLAND CELEBRATES AFTER SCORING A GOAL DURING THE FIFA 2002 WORLD CUP QUALIFIER AGAINST GERMANY PLAYED AT THE OLYMPIC STADIUM IN MUNICH, GERMANY. ENGLAND WON THE MATCH 5-1

PHOTO: BEN RADFORD/ALLSPORT UK/GETTY IMAGES

1 SEPTEMBER 2001: ENGLAND ARE WELL ON THEIR WAY TO VICTORY IN THE
FIFA 2002 WORLD CUP QUALIFIER BETWEEN GERMANY AND ENGLAND. ENGLAND WON THE MATCH 5-1
PHOTO: SHAUN BOTTERILL/ALLSPORT UK/GETTY IMAGES

17 JUNE 2004: WAYNE ROONEY OF ENGLAND CELEBRATES AFTER SCORING DURING THE UEFA EURO 2004 GROUP B MATCH
BETWEEN ENGLAND AND SWITZERLAND AT THE ESTADIO CIDADE DE COIMBRA, PORTUGAL
PHOTO: SHAUN BOTTERILL/GETTY IMAGES

JOHN TERRY, MICHAEL OWEN AND DAVID BECKHAM HELP UNVEIL THE NEW ENGLAND FOOTBALL AWAY KIT INSPIRED BY THE CLASSIC 1966 DESIGN
AND TO BE WORN AGAINST URUGUAY ON MARCH 1 FOR THE WORLD CUP WARM-UP MATCH. SAS RADISSON MANCHESTER AIRPORT HOTEL, MANCHESTER. 27 FEBRUARY 2006
PHOTO: RALPH PETTS/PN NEWS/LFI

England Crazy

Words & Music by
Michael Harwood, Nicholas Keynes, Jon O'Mahony, T. Sutterby, Toby Orme,
Anthony Miller, Jeremy Huffelman, J. Pearson & Leo Green

Ev-'ry-bo-dy loves___ you, ba- by; we're all go-ing Eng- land cra- zy.

Vindaloo

Words & Music by
Keith Allen, Guy Pratt & Alex James

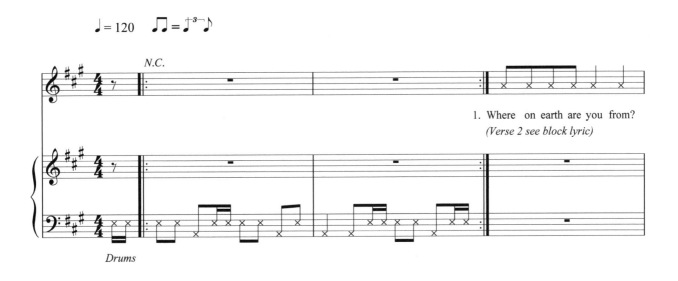

1. Where on earth are you from?
(Verse 2 see block lyric)

Drums

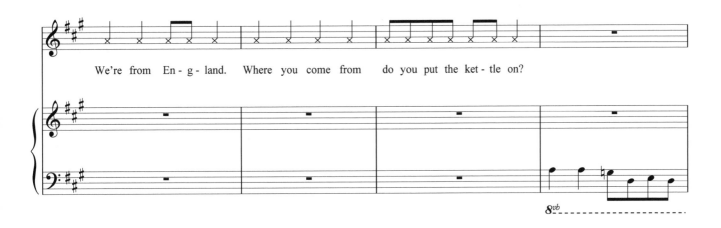

We're from En - g - land. Where you come from do you put the ket - tle on?

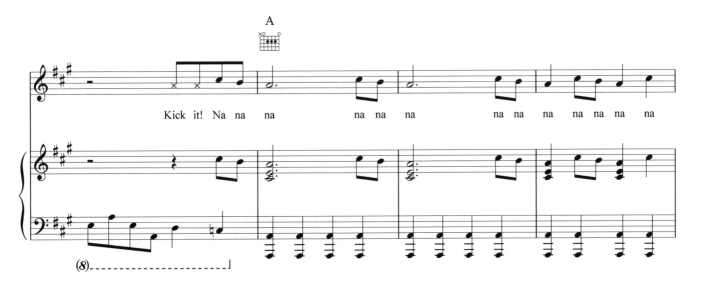

Kick it! Na na na na na na na na na na na na na

Verse 2
Can I introduce you please
To a lump of cheddar cheese?
Knit one, purl one
Drop one, curl one.

Kick it! Na na na *etc.*

Three Lions

Words by David Baddiel & Frank Skinner
Music by Ian Broudie

Repeat and fade

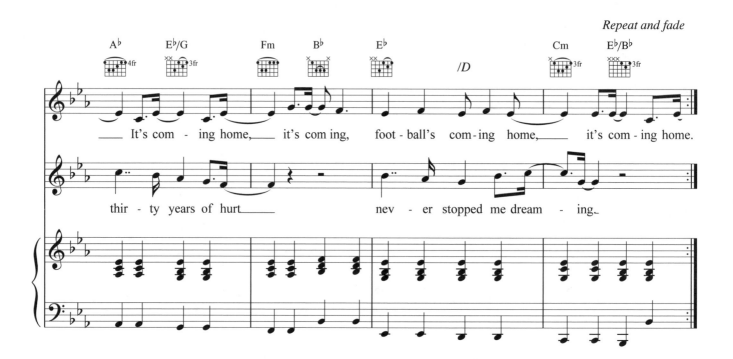

Verse 2:
So many jokes, so many sneers,
But all those oh-so-nears
Wear yóu down
Through the years.
But I still see that tackle by Moore
And when Lineker scored,
Bobby belting the ball
And Nobby dancing.

This Time (We'll Get It Right)

Words & Music by
Christopher Norman & Peter Spencer